NICK BUTTERWORTH AND MICK INKPEN

# STORIES JESUS TOLD

To help people understand what God is like,
Jesus told lots of stories which are as exciting
today as when they were first heard.

*The Rich Farmer* is still a great favourite
and its message is one that children especially
love to hear.

Marshall Pickering
An Imprint of HarperCollins*Publishers*
77-85 Fulham Palace Road,
Hammersmith, London W6 8JB
1 3 5 7 9 10 8 6 4 2

First published in Great Britain
in 1989 by Marshall Pickering

This edition published in 1995

A catalogue record for this book is
available from the British Library

0 551 02880-7

Printed and bound in Hong Kong

Co-edition arranged by Angus Hudson Ltd, London

# The Rich Farmer

## Nick Butterworth and Mick Inkpen

HarperCollins*Publishers*

Here is a farmer who is
very rich. The farmer is rich
because his soil is rich.
And his corn grows faster
than anyone else's.

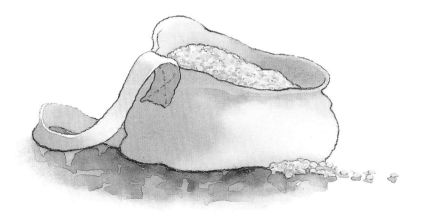

And higher than anyone else's.

And at harvest time he has much more of it than anyone else! Lucky man.

This year he has so much corn
that his old barn can't hold it all.
It is bursting at the seams.

'No problem,' says the farmer.
'I will pull it down and build
a bigger one. Then next year I
will be rich enough to take
life easy.'

So he builds a bigger barn.

But when harvest comes round again, the new barn is not big enough.

The greedy farmer has planted more corn than before. And carrots too.

'No problem,' says the farmer.
'I will build an even bigger,
better barn. Then next year I
will be richer still and then
I can really enjoy myself.'

So he builds a bigger, better
barn.

But at harvest time, even the bigger, better barn is not big enough.

Again the farmer has planted too much corn, too many carrots. (And a few cabbages as well.)

This time, the farmer says to himself, 'I will build the biggest, grandest barn the world has ever seen. And then I shall be so rich, I need never work again!'

The barn he builds reaches
up to the sky. When it is
finished the farmer sighs a
great big sigh.

'Tomorrow I will gather in the
harvest and then at last I shall
begin to enjoy myself. I know!
I'll have a party!'

But that very night he dies
in his sleep. Just like that!

The birds eat his corn,
the rabbits dig up his carrots
and his cabbages go to seed.

The big barn stands empty
and the rich farmer never does
get to enjoy his money.

Poor man.

Jesus says, 'How silly it is for a man to spend his whole life storing up riches for himself. To God, he is really a poor man.'

You can read the story of
*The Rich Farmer* in Luke
chapter 12 verses 13 to 21.

*If you enjoyed this story, why not try*
*other titles in the* Stories Jesus Told *series*
*by Nick Butterworth and Mick Inkpen*

The Good Stranger
The House On The Rock
The Little Gate
The Lost Sheep
The Precious Pearl
The Ten Silver Coins
The Two Sons

*Other well-known Bible stories are retold by*
*Nick Butterworth and Mick Inkpen in the delightful*
Animal Tales *series*

The Cat's Tale
The Fox's Tale
The Magpie's Tale
The Mouse's Tale